Volume
1

Juz 'Amma

For School Students

Workbook

Fatima Meghezzi El-Hindi

Taqwa
PRINTS

May Allāh bless my parents for their assistance, guidance and inspiration, my father and mother in-law for their support and special thanks to my husband for his patience.

Fatima Meghezzi El-Hindi,

ISBN 13: 978-1-936569-29-8

First edition: 2014
Reprint: 2017, 2019

Taqwa Prints
5584 Boulder Crest St.
Columbus, OH 43235
www.taqwaprints.com

Printed in China

Price: US $6.00

Preface

At relatively young age, most Muslim children memorize a few sūrah from the 30th part of the Qur'ān—also known as Juz Amma. As they progress in age and grade, many of them continue memorizing additional sūrah. There are quite a few student-friendly Juz Amma books in the market, catering to the needs of our young learners. Many of them seem to facilitate memorizing the sūrah, some focus on understanding the meanings of the sūrahs, and a few others seem to provide additional resources. The overall objective of all the books is to help young children to better understand the holy book of guidance in simple language and concepts that they can follow. However, none of the books seemed to provide quality homework or learning activities based on the sūrah. I always felt something has to be done to make learning more interesting and encouraging.

Now a days, the teaching methodologies have changed. Teachers want the students to learn, but with plenty of fun. When it comes to learning the Qur'ān, the fun part seems to be a taboo thing. However, the fun part can be done in a respectful manner without lowering the dignity of the book of guidance—the Qur'ān.

From my personal experiences as a child, I remember, I did not understand what we were memorizing in the Qur'ān. I always felt that if this great book is the guidance for daily life then we need to be able to understand it at a young age rather than just memorizing for use in the prayers only. That need became more apparent to me when I was teaching my own children. As the director of NAS Learning Center, Syracuse, NY, I spent a great deal of time looking for books to satisfy that need. Unfortunately we could only find learning materials suitable for middle school age kids or older, while kids in grades 1 – 5 were lacking books appropriate for their age.

With the help of Allāh and Sheikh Mohamed Al-Ghazali's advice (may Allah bless him), I decided to put together a series of Qur'ānic activity and workbooks that will be suitable and effective for young children. My objective was to make children develop a good feelings about the Qur'ān and love it. I produced locally printed workbooks for my students at the NAS Learning Center. The workbooks were deeply appreciated by our teachers and parents.

In the meantime, I was discussing the scope of publishing the workbook with Brother Husain Nuri. The idea was to make the workbook as an addendum of his textbook, Juz Amma for School Students. He suggested to add additional activities and have a layout artist design the entire book. The idea was to make the workbook more effective for a wider range of school students. With his help, I have updated and modified the manuscript to make it more appealing. At this time, only volume 1 of the workbook, covering up to sūrah Al-Qadr is being published. Insha-Allah volume 2 will be published at a later time. While preparing the manuscript, I have benefited immensely from my students, teachers and my children. I appreciate their support, encouragement and criticism. I sincerely hope that this workbook will benefit our students and teachers. If there is any good and benefit in this work, it is due to Allāh and all shortcomings are solely mine.

June 1, 2014   Fatima Meghezzi El-Hindi

Acknowledgment

The author of this book would like to thank all those who helped with feedback and comments particularly members of the NAS Learning Center teaching staff.

We also give thanks to all our darling students at NAS Learning Center who were the first to use the book activities and showed us how enjoyable and successful this book can be for loving and learning Qur'ān.

Special acknowledgement goes to Nour Sahraoui and the team of Weekend Learning Publishers, particularly Husain A. Nuri who assisted with compiling the activities and Authoug Atieh for editing the book.

Table of Contents

Sūrah 1

Revealed in Makkah

Al-Fātihah

The Opening

Review Summary

Sūrah *Al-Fātihah* has seven āyāt. Placed at the beginning of the Qur'ān, this sūrah is very special and actually a prayer. Sūrah Al-Fātiha is also called Umu Al-Kitāb. In this sūrah, Allāh ﷻ teaches us to ask for guidance in this life and to be good, not like those who tend to make him angry. Allāhﷻ promises to give us whatever we ask for because He is surely kind and loves us.

Review Questions

1. What is the meaning of the word Fātihah?

   The Opening

2. What is another name of Sūrah *Al-Fātihah*?

3. How many āyāt or verses do Sūrah *Al-Fātihah* have?

   7

4. Which āyah of Sūrah *Al-Fātihah* is the longest? Write the āyah number.

   7

5. Read the first āyah of Sūrah Al-Fātihah. What belongs to Allāh?

The prayers belong to Allah.

6. What two names of Allāh are mentioned in āyah 2 of Sūrah Al-Fātihah.

ar-Rahman & ar Rahim

7. Read āyah 6 of Sūrah Al-Fātihah. What type of path do we want to follow?

Right Path

8. Search the following words in the word maze.

SURAH   FATIHAH   ALLAH   GUIDE   PATH   WORSHIP   PRAISE

A	W	O	R	S	H	I	P	T
F	G	S	R	O	S	U	A	K
A	H	U	F	G	P	U	T	F
T	W	R	E	S	R	D	H	A
I	R	A	L	L	A	H	Y	R
H	T	H	P	L	I	B	S	A
A	K	L	L	E	S	N	C	O
H	G	U	I	D	E	H	U	M

9. Connect the dots. Color the shape.

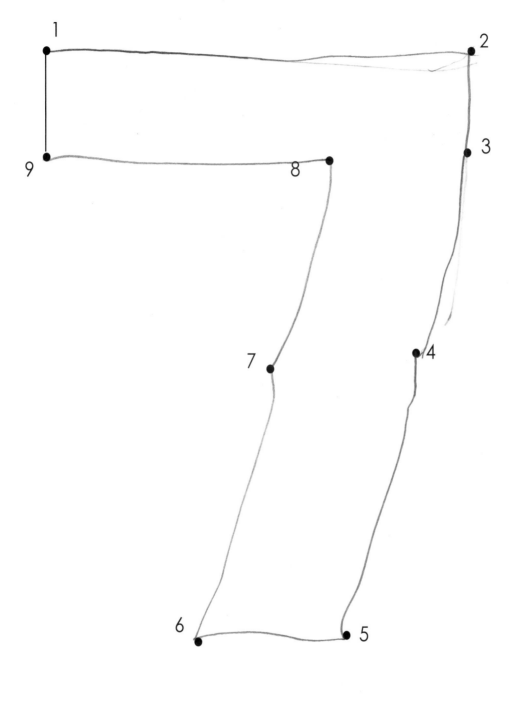

How do the shape relate to the Sūrah Al-Fātihah?

7 āyahs

10. Unscramble the following words to make meaningful words.

RPAREY   P R A Y E R

AALHL   A L L A H

BITAK   K I T A B

TAFIHHA   F A T I I H A H

Now write the letters in the boxes to make a secret word.

The secret word is: P A T H

In which āyah in Sūrah Al-Fātihah can you find the mention of the secret word that you solved above? Write the āyah number.

Ayah 6

11. Circle **T** if the sentence is true. Circle **F** is the sentence is false.

Allāh is the Master of the Day of Judgment.   (T)   F

All praise belongs to the angels.   T   (F)

We ask Allāh to guide us in a Straight Path.   (T)   F

People who walked on the Straight Path were favored.   T   (F)

Some people were lost because they took the Straight Path.   T   (F)

Allāh is is the Lord of this earth, but not the other worlds.   T   (F)

12. Fill in the blanks using the appropriate words for the box.

> guidance   help   Master   anger   worlds

Ayah 5 says, we worship Allāh and seek His _help_.

Allāh is the _Master_ of the Day of Judgment.

Allāh is the Lord of all the _worlds_.

Those who do not walk on the Straight Path earn _anger_.

The message of Sūrah Al-Fātihah is to seek _guidance_.

Juz 'Amma

Revealed in Makkah

An-Nās

Mankind

Review Summary

This is the ending sūrah of the Majestic Qur'ān. In this sūrah, we declare Allāh as the Lord and Master of Mankind. The main point of this sūrah is to always ask Allāh for protection because he is the Almighty that has control over everything.

Shaitan is our biggest enemy. He whispers to us because he wants us to do wrong things, and then runs away. That is why we should ask Allāh to protect us from him! Shaitan wants our hearts to become filled with evil so that we will do bad things. Allāh teaches us to seek shelter with Him and ask for His protection from the evils of Jinn and bad people.

Review Questions

1. What is the first Arabic word in sūrah an-Nās?

....

2. In the first āyah of sūrah an-Nās, what are we seeking from our Rabb?

....

3. What are some of the meanings of the word "Rabb" ?

....

....

....

4. From what things do we seek refuge with Allāh ?

....

5. In āyah 4, what name is used for Shaitan?

....

6. How does Shaitan puts evil thoughts in our minds?

....

7. What are the two sources from which bad thoughts enter in our hearts?

....

....

8. At what time of the day should we recite sūrah an-Nās? Color the correct box.

| Morning | Noon | Evening | Anytime |

9. When do you think sūrah an-Nās protects you? Color the correct box.

| At home | At school | During sleep | At all the time |

10. What is the sūrah number for an-Nās?

....

11. How many sūrah are there in the Qur'ān?

....

12. Complete the puzzle with the clues given below:

Across:

2. The evil-one does this to our hearts.
5. We get bad thoughts from them.
6. We should put ____ bad thoughts from coming to our minds.
7. Arabic for God.

Down:

1. This word is used as a name for Shaitan in sūrah an-Nās.
3. Shaitan always influences them.
4. When bad thoughts appear, we seek this with Allāh.

13. Find the following words **two times** in the word maze.

> RABB   MALIK   REFUGE   HEARTS

```
M  E  R  A  B  B  C  R
A  A  E  E  S  M  N  E
L  W  F  T  H  A  H  F
I  D  U  L  G  L  E  U
K  E  G  K  B  I  A  G
M  T  E  L  I  K  R  E
H  E  A  R  T  S  T  K
P  R  A  B  B  D  S  A
```

14. Write the meaning of the following words used in sūrah an-Nas.

إِلَه   ....

شَرِّ   ....

مَلِك   ....

15. Following sentence are either true or false. Circle the letter under True, if the sentence is true. Circle the letter under False if the sentence is not true.

	TRUE	FALSE
The word Rabb generally means Lord	P	C
Allāh﷾ has a few children.	G	R
The word Mālik means king.	O	Z
You do not need God's help to protect yourself.	H	T
The word ilah means God.	E	M
Allāh﷾ is the Master of mankind.	C	P
Shaitān tells us to do good things.	Q	T
Bad ideas come to us from Jinn and people.	O	W
Sūrah an-Nās is the last sūrah in the Qur'ān.	R	S

Now write the circled letters below.

— — — — — — — — —

The above word best describes someone. Write His name below.

....

Sūrah 113 | Al-Falaq
The Daybreak

Revealed in Makkah

Review Summary

Allāh☝ created everything in this world for our benefit. If we do not use His creations properly, they can become evil. In this sūrah, Allāh☝ teaches us to seek protection with Him from the evils that people create and the mischief of black magic. The sūrah also teaches us to seek protection from those who are jealous of us and from those who want to harm us due to their jealousy.

Review Questions

1. What is the meaning of the word falaq?

   ....

2. What quality of Allāh☝ is mentioned in āyah 1 of sūrah al-Falaq?

   ....

3. Read āyah 3 of sūrah al-Falaq. Explain some of the meaning of darkness mentioned in this āyah.

   ....

   ....

4. How many types of mischief or evil does sūrah al-Falaq mention?

....

5, Before Islam, people in Arabia practiced black magic. Give an examples of their black magic.

....

6. Color all the pictures below. Then cross out the ones from which you seek Allāh's protection.

7. Fill in the blanks using the words in the box.

jealous	darkness	evil
Rabb	magic	daybreak

Say, I seek refuge with the .... of the .... from the .... of what He has created, namely from the evil of the .... when it spreads, and from the evil of .... and from the evil of the .... people when they begin to dislike and hate us.

8. When people envy us, what two things they do that harms others? Write your answer based on the explanation of āyah 5.

They become ....

They become ....

9. Write the meaning of the following words:

ٱلْفَلَقِ ....

خَلَقَ ....

شَرِّ ....

10. Find the following words in the word maze.

| DARK | DAYBREAK | JEALOUS | FALAQ | ENVY |
| HAPPY | KNOTS | MAGIC | REFUGE | EVIL |

```
M  A  T  I  C  A  E  J  T
B  N  E  V  I  L  R  E  S
P  D  A  Y  B  R  E  A  K
F  A  L  A  Q  R  F  L  G
X  R  A  E  U  D  U  O  M
S  K  Y  A  V  A  G  U  A
H  O  E  N  V  Y  E  S  G
H  A  P  P  Y  T  U  F  I
E  A  G  K  N  O  T  S  C
```

Sūrah 112

Revealed in Makkah

Al-Ikhlās

The Unity of Allāh ﷻ

Review Summary

In this sūrah we learned that Allāh ﷻ is one and unique. There is nothing like Him anywhere.

- Allāh ﷻ has no children, therefore, He is not a parent
- Allāh ﷻ was never born and He will never die.
- No one or nothing is like Allāh ﷻ.

Review Questions

1. What is the main theme of sūrah al-Ikhlās?

   ....

2. What are the two names of Allāh ﷻ mentioned in sūrah al-Ikhlās?

   ....

3. What is the meaning of the word as-Samad?

   ....

4. Explain the meaning of the third āyah in sūrah al-Ikhlās?

   ....

   ....

5. Rearrange the jumbled letter to make meaningful words.

A D H A   __ __ __ __

A S D A M   __ __ __ __ __

A H L A L   __ __ __ __ __

6. Write five things about Allāhﷻ that we learned from sūrah al-Ikhlās.

a. ....

b. ....

c. ....

d. ....

e. ....

7. Write the meaning of the following words:

هُوَ   ....

لَمْ   ....

كُفُوًا   ....

أَحَدٌ   ....

8. Color the number and the word below.

In sūrah al-Ikhlās, we learned Allāh is One.

9. Color the statement below.

We worship
Only
Allah

10. Circle T if the sentence is correct. Circle F if the sentence is false.

Allāh is one.   T   F

To beget means to give birth.   T   F

Jesus is Allāh's only begotten son.   T   F

Muhammad (S) is equal to Allāh.   T   F

To compare anything as equal or similar to Allāh is a sin.   T   F

11. Find as many words of three or more letters from this wordwheel. Form words by using the letter in the center of the wheel plus a selection from the outer wheel. No letters may be used for more than once in a word, except if a letter is present twice in the outer wheel.

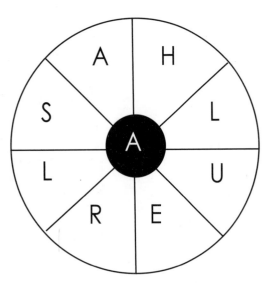

Sūrah 111 | Al-Masad/Al-Lahab

Revealed in Makkah

The Palm Fiber/The Firebrand

Review Summary

In this sūrah we learn about hatred of Abu Lahab and his wife toward Islam and Muslims. Abu Lahab was Rasūlullāh's 🕌 uncle. He did not accept Islam. He and his wife used to harass Rasūlullāh🕌 and his followers. Allāh🕌 promises to punish Abu Lahab and his wife for their harmful activities.

- Their wealth and children will not be able to help them.
- Abu Lahab will be thrown into Hell Fire.
- His wife will have a rope of rough palm leaves around her neck.

Review Questions

1. Who was Abu Lahab?

   ....

2. What was Abu Lahab's actual name?

   ....

3. Who in Abu Lahab's family used to harass Rasūlullāh🕌?

   ....

4. Each of the questions below is followed by two or three choices. Color the box that has the correct answer.

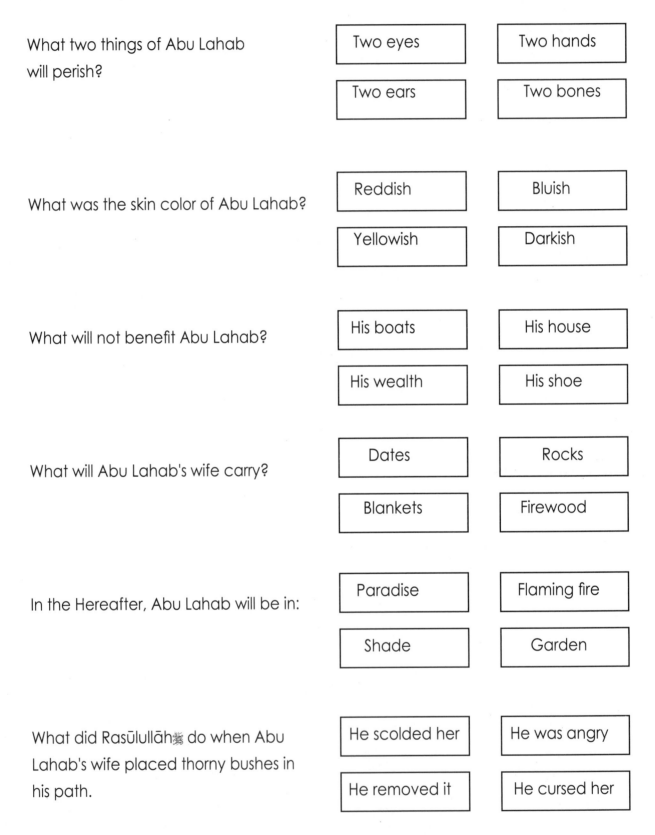

What two things of Abu Lahab will perish?

| Two eyes | Two hands |
| Two ears | Two bones |

What was the skin color of Abu Lahab?

| Reddish | Bluish |
| Yellowish | Darkish |

What will not benefit Abu Lahab?

| His boats | His house |
| His wealth | His shoe |

What will Abu Lahab's wife carry?

| Dates | Rocks |
| Blankets | Firewood |

In the Hereafter, Abu Lahab will be in:

| Paradise | Flaming fire |
| Shade | Garden |

What did Rasūlullāhﷺ do when Abu Lahab's wife placed thorny bushes in his path.

| He scolded her | He was angry |
| He removed it | He cursed her |

5. How will Abu Lahab's wife be punished?

....

....

6. What is another meaning of the word "hands" of Abu Lahab?

....

7. Fill in the blanks with the understood meanings from sūrah Masad.

Abu Lahab's wife will have ropes around her ....

Abu Lahab will be .... in the flame of fire.

The .... of Abu Lahab will not benefit him in anyway.

The real name of Abu Lahab was ....

Abu Lahab's wife's name was ....

8. What was the relationship between Rasūlullāh and Abu Lahab?

Rasūlullāh was Abu Lahab's ....

Abu Lahab was Rasūlullāh's ....

9. Choose five words from the following list to fill Abu Lahab's hand with behavior that destroyed him.

> greed   truthful   liar   mean   kind   helpful   tricky   jealous

10. Draw a line from the Arabic word to its meaning.

مَالُهُۥ	to him
يَدَآ	fire
عَنْهُ	wealth
نَارًا	two hands
وَٱمْرَأَتُهُۥ	rope
كَسَبَ	firewood
ٱلْحَطَبِ	his wife
حَبْلٌ	he earned

Sūrah 110

An-Nasr

The Help

Review Summary

This sūrah was the last complete sūrah revealed to our Rasūlullāhﷺ. It was revealed shortly after his Hajj in the 10th year of *Hijrah*. It was the one and only Hajj of Rasūlullāhﷺ.

About 100,000 people attended Hajj that year. Large number of people already accepted Islam and many more began to accept Islam. Muslims had already achieved victory in battles and almost all of Arabia had accepted Islam. Such a large Muslim population reminded everyone about the victory of Islam. The victory was a result of the help of Allāhﷻ.

On seeing the victory of Islam, we should not become proud. This sūrah reminds all of us to stay humble and continue praising Allāhﷻ and continue asking for forgiveness for errors or mistakes in life.

Review Questions

1. What two things does Allāhﷻ tell us to do after we win?

   ....

   ....

2. When was the sūrah an-Nasr revealed?

   ....

3. What is the meaning of "istighfar"?

   ....

4. At the time of Rasūlullāh, after Muslims achieved victory, what were they doing?

   (a) They began leaving Islam.
   (b) They began worshipping other gods.
   (c) They began accepting Islam.
   (d) They began glorifying Muhammad.

5. The last revealed sūrah was an-Nasr. When was this sūrah revealed?

   (a) At the time of Hijrat of Rasūlullāh.
   (b) After Muslims defeated the Quraish in a battle near Madinah.
   (c) After Rasūlullāh performed umrah in 630 C.E.
   (d) After the only Hajj of Rasūlullāh, about two months before his death.

6. Color the following words:

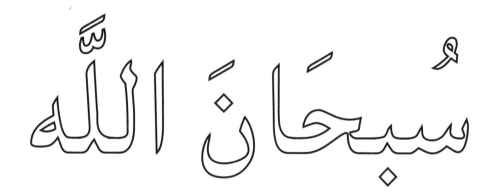

Sūrah an-Nasr teaches us to say these two words whenever we win.

7. Color the Ka'bah.

In 630 C.E., eight years after Hijrah, Rasūlullāh﷽ returned to Makkah as a winner. He purified the Ka'bah from idol worshippers.

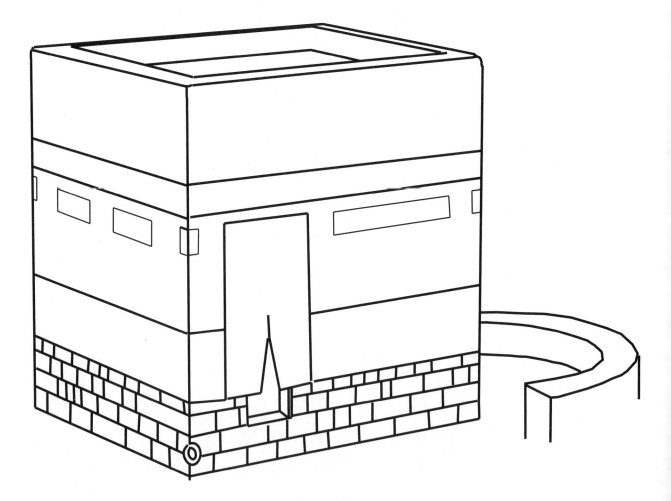

8. Cut all the words from the bottom of the page and paste them in appropriate blanks of sūrah an-Nasr.

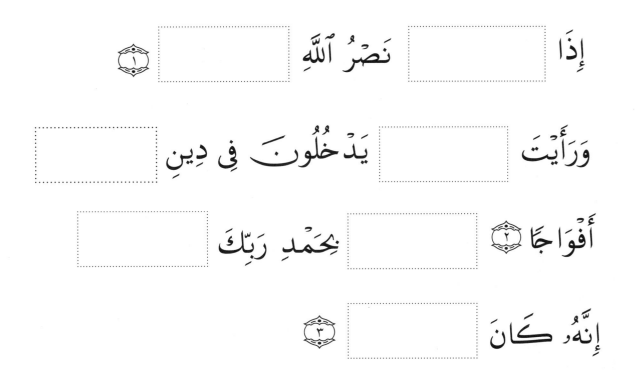

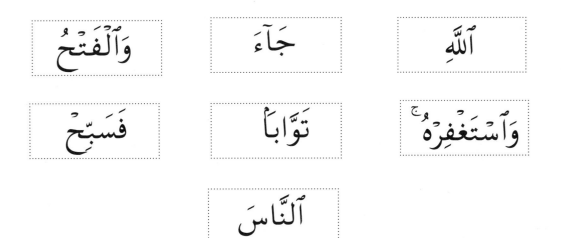

This page is blank for the cutting activity on the opposite side.

Sūrah 109
Revealed in Makkah
Al-Kāfirūn
The Nonbelievers

Review Summary

A few people from Makkah suggested that they would worship Allāh for one year if Rasūlullāh worshipped their idols for the next year. Allāh then revealed this sūrah to make it clear that this was an impossible idea.

Islam is a religion of tolerance. Islam teaches that in the matter of faith, no one should force another person. Everyone has the right to practice their own religion. We should not argue but simply say, "I have my way and you have yours." This sūrah tells Rasūlullāh and all of us that we cannot compromise the truth. It is Allāh who will judge truth from falsehood on the Day of Judgment.

Review Questions

1. Why was sūrah al-Kafirun sent to Rasūlullāh ?

   ....

   ....

2. How does Allāh teach us to answer the people who may ask us to leave Islam and follow another religion?

   ....

   ....

3. Sūrah Al-Kafirun teaches us: (circle the correct answer)

    (a) Be tolerant to others.

    (b) To never give up our own faith.

    (c) Love the idols just like we love Allāh.

    (d) Never use force in the religion.

    (e) Worship some good idols but avoid bad ones.

    (f) The paths of idol-worshippers are totally different from Islam.

4. Eight words are given in the box. Pick the correct words to complete the sentences below.

Idols	worship	kafir	life
physical	force	path	other

In the matter of religion there is no .... to believe.

In the beginning many of the Quraish loved to worship their ....

Many of the Quraish wanted to see their god in .... form.

Rasulullah would not .... what the Quraish worship.

A .... is a person who refuses to believe and reject faith.

Muslims do not follow the .... of the idol-worshippers.

The meaning of Arabic word "din" is a way of ....

The Quraish asked Rasulullah to worship their idols in every ....
year, and they would worship his God in return.

5. Complete the puzzle using the clues given below.

Across:

1. Muslims and non-Muslims do this to different god.

4. The *ilah* of the Muslims.

5. Muslims never _____ up their faith.

6. This is not applied in religion.

Down:

2. This is different for Muslims and non-Muslims.

3. Non-Muslim's _____ is different from ours. Also means road.

6. Color the following pictures. In the box next to each picture, write the first letter of the name of the picture.

2 ☐

1 ☐

3 ☐

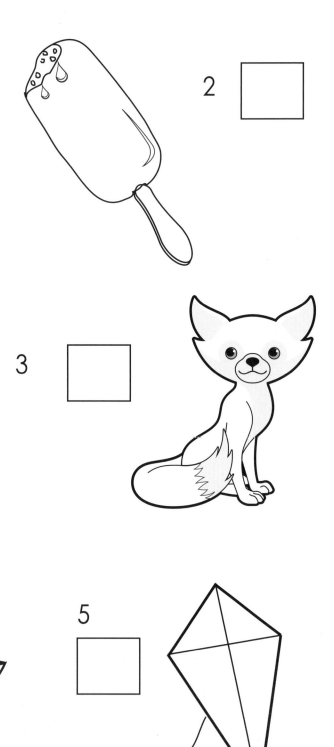

4 ☐

5 ☐

6 ☐

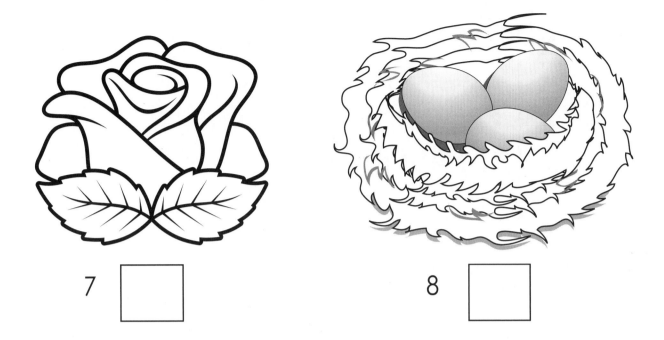

7 ☐   8 ☐

Now on the lines below, a number is indicated for the respective letter. Write the corresponding letter to find a meaningful word.

   6   1   5   6   3   2   7   4   8

Sūrah 108

Al-Kawthar

The Abundance

Review Summary

When Rasūlullāh lost his son Qasim, some of the people of Quraish made fun of him. They said that no one will carry his name. Allāh revealed this sūrah with a promise to Rasūlullāh that he will never be forgotten. On the other hand, those who hate Rasūlullāh will not be remembered.

This short sūrah tells us to be thankful to Allāh for His blessings upon us. The best way to show that we are thankful to Allāh is to perform salāt and to sacrifice.

Review Questions

1. According to sūrah al-Kawthar, who will lose in the end?

....

2. Why was sūrah al-Kawthar revealed to Rasūlullāh?

....

....

3. What does Allāh ask Rasūlullāh and us to do when we thank Him for his favors?

....

....

4. Find the following words in the word maze. Search the words in all directions, including backwards and diagonally.

kawthar	sacrifice	paradise	river	jealous
envy	salat	qasim	hereafter	

L V O I G D P J W V Y E

S A C Q B Q A S I M Y O

W P A R V M R R M Z G F

N G G Y K T A L A S B A

F N V N C H D R M Z B X

J N C M T C I T I U U Q

E C Y W S K S I K V J U

V L A H E R E A F T E R

K K W J E A L U R M C R

R T O L J E A L O U S C

E C I F I R C A S P Q W

P Q R E L I G I O N U A

Bonus word: **RELIGION**

5. Six words are given in the box. Pick the correct words to complete the sentences below.

> hereafter   sacrifice   world
>
> salat   al-kawthar   hate

A special river in paradise is named as... .

When believers receive good in this word they are required to perform

.... and do ....

Allāh gives us good in this .... and will give more good in

the ....

Those who .... us will cut off from all good things in this life an

in the hereafter .

6. Write the meaning of the following words.

اَنْحَر   = ...

اِنَّ   = ...

بَتَرَ   = ...

7. Mention five blessings that you received in your life or in your family life.

....

....

....

....

....

8. Unscramble the following to make meaningful words.

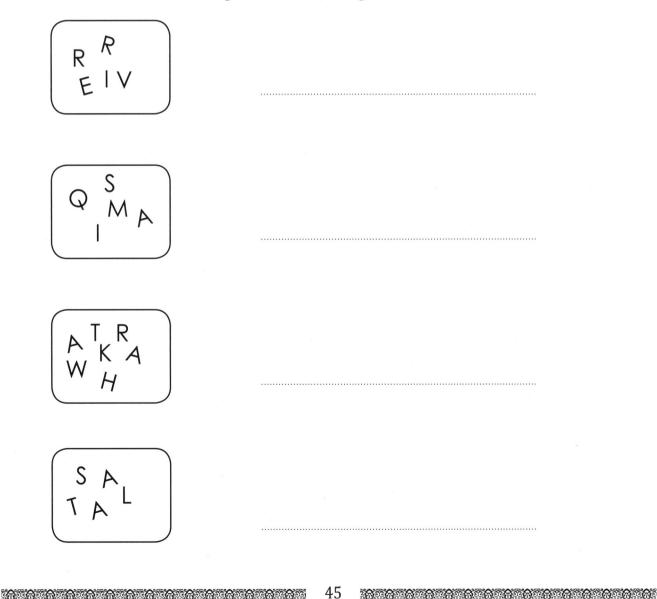

R R E I V ....

Q S I M A ....

A T R K A W H ....

S A L T A ....

Sūrah 107

Revealed in Makkah

Al-Mā'ùn

The Acts of Kindness

Review Summary

This sūrah discusses people who deny two things—(1) the teachings of the religion, and (2) the duty to help the poor. These people think they are following Islam, but they neglect the poor and orphans. They perform prayers but are careless about the prayers. They only pray for show and refuse to do the smallest kindness to others. Therefore, Allāh does not like them.

Review Questions

1. Mention 3 negative qualities of the type of person mentioned in sūrah al-Mā'ūn.

....

....

....

2. What does the person in sūrah al-Mā'ūn do to the orphans?

....

3. What does the person in sūrah al-Mā'ūn do during salāt?

....

4. What could be the reason the person in sūrah al-Mā'ūn does not want to feed the poor?

   ....

5. Write the meaning of the following words:

يَتِيْم   = ...

مِسْكِيْن   = ...

دِيْن   = ...

مُصَلِّيْن   = ...

6. Each of the questions below is followed by two or three choices. Color the box that has the correct answer.

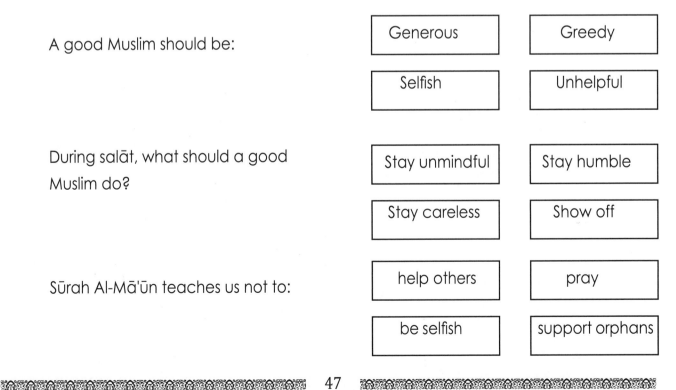

A good Muslim should be:

| Generous | Greedy |
| Selfish | Unhelpful |

During salāt, what should a good Muslim do?

| Stay unmindful | Stay humble |
| Stay careless | Show off |

Sūrah Al-Mā'ūn teaches us not to:

| help others | pray |
| be selfish | support orphans |

7. Fill in the blanks with appropriate words to find out the things that good Muslims should or should not do.

> Orphan   poor   prayers   help   greedy   liked
> chase   Show off   follow   Day of Judgment

Muslims should believe in the ....

Muslims should be kind to the ....

Muslims should provide food for the needy and the ....

Muslims do their .... the proper way.

Muslims do not like to .... during salāt or at other time.

Muslims should always .... others as much as they can.

Muslims .... the teachings of the religion properly.

A good Muslim should not be ....

If orphans or needy people come to good Muslim, they should not

.... they away.

Careless and showy salāt are not .... by Allāh .

8. Complete the puzzle using the clues given below.

Across:

1. A good Muslims will never do this to a poor or to an orphan. Talk bad.

3. To orphans we should do this.

6. It would be bad to leave the orphans in this condition. It occurs in the stomach.

Down:

1. People do not feed the orphans because they are _____

2. Follow His instructions. The Rabb.

4. Follow His instruction or _____ His anger. Also means income.

5. Allāh does not like if we do this in a proud manner. Worship.

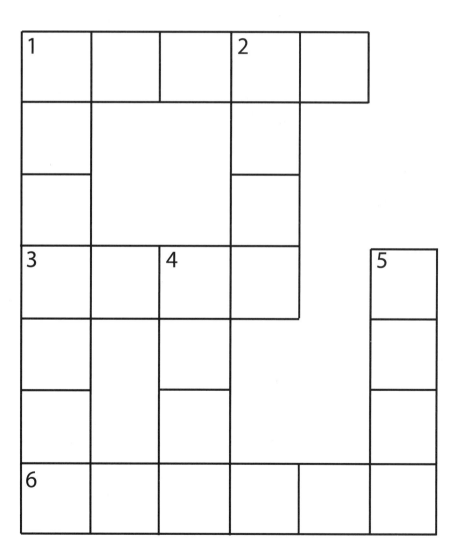

9. Find the following words in the word maze. Search the words in all directions, including backwards and diagonally.

careless	orphan	guidance	forgetful	surah
ignore	feed	kindness	poor	salat

```
A  A  N  O  X  M  P  L  G  C  C  N
N  F  E  P  E  W  G  B  L  E  K  K
A  E  R  Y  K  F  F  B  S  U  Q  I
H  E  T  A  L  A  S  S  U  G  X  N
P  D  L  U  F  T  E  G  R  O  F  D
R  E  Z  S  I  P  K  B  A  S  C  N
O  E  N  J  R  T  F  B  H  B  X  E
H  T  K  G  U  I  D  A  N  C  E  S
Y  A  L  M  A  U  N  E  Z  P  Y  S
H  V  J  R  Q  E  N  R  O  O  P  F
Z  N  S  S  E  L  E  R  A  C  E  Y
I  G  N  O  R  E  M  C  Q  I  P  O
```

Bonus word: **al maun**

Sūrah 106

Revealed in Makkah

Quraish

Review Summary

The Quraish were one of the major tribes that lived in Mecca at the time of Rasūlullāh ﷺ. They were respected by other tribes because they were the caretakers of the Ka'bah. Because of this, many of the Quraish became proud. They refused to listen to the message of Rasūlullāh ﷺ.

Mecca is a mountainous place, in the middle of the desert. Almost nothing grows in Makkah. The people of Makkah used to travel to Yemen for trade in the winter months and to Syria during the summer. The trade activities made them rich. In this sūrah, Allāh ﷻ tells them to worship Him and be grateful to Him because He is the one who provided for them, and protected them during their trade journey.

Review Questions

1. Who or what were the Quraish?

   ....

2. Which two places did the Quraish travel to do trade activities?

   ....

3. What reasons did Allāh ﷻ provide the Quraish asking them to worship Him?

   ....

   ....

4. Mention some of the blessings the Quraish received from Allāh﷾ .

....

....

5. Why would no Arab tribes attacked the Quraish during their trade journey?

....

6. What were some of the travel related dangers that all Arab tribes faced?

....

....

7. There is a mention of "house" in sūrah Quraish. Whose house is it?

....

8. Draw lines from the Arabic words used in sūrah al-Quraish to their meanings.

ٱلشِّتَآءِ   Hunger

وَٱلصَّيْفِ   Fear

ٱلْبَيْتِ   The winter

جُوعٍ   The summer

خَوْفٍ   The house

9. In the two rectangles, write the names of two places where the Quraish traveled to do trade activities in the summer and winter. Then color the two camels.

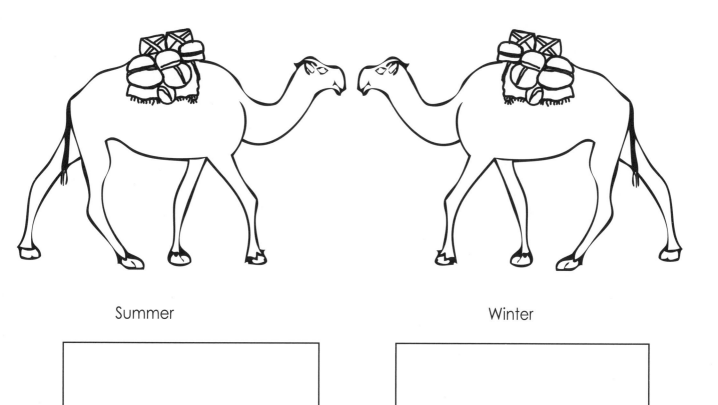

Summer

Winter

10. Makkah is a rocky, mountainous place with no agriculture. How did the Quraish get food in such a place?

....

11. In the beginning, the Quraish did not believe in Allāh. Yet why did Allāh feed them and protect them?

....

....

12. Unscramble the following words to make meaningful words.

Y S A R I   ☐ __ __ __ ☐

M N E E Y   __ __ __ __ __

N I T W R E   __ __ __ __ __ ☐

U G H N R E   ☐ ☐ __ __ __ __

Now rearrange the letters in the boxes to make a secret word.

The secret word is: __ __ __ __ __

13. Circle T if the sentence is correct. Circle F if the sentence is false.

The Quraish traveled to China and Yemen to do trades.   T   F

The reason Allāh﷾ protected the Quraish is because they   T   F
always worshipped Allāh﷾ .

Many of the Arab tribes attacked the Quraish during their travel.   T   F

The Quraish were caretaker of the Ka'bah, therefore, people   T   F
respected them.

The Quraish became rich due to their trade activities.   T   F

The Lord of the House is none but Allāh﷾ .   T   F

The Quraish were asked to worship the Lord of the House.   T   F

Sūrah 105

Revealed in Makkah

Al-Fil

The Elephant

Review **Summary**

This sūrah tells the story of Allāh saving the Ka'bah from the evil plots of enemies. This incident happened the year rasūl Muhammad (S) was born. A Christian ruler named Abrahah attacked Makkah with large African elephants in order to destroy the Ka'bah. Before Abrahah could harm the Ka'bah, Allāh destroyed his army in a dramatic manner. Allāh sent a large number of birds to destroy the army. The army was also knocked out with stones of baked clay and became like the chewed-up straw from which grains had been eaten away.

Review **Questions**

1. Who was Abrahah?

....

2. Why did Abrahah come to Makkah? (circle the correct answer)

(a) He wanted to rebuild the Ka'bah.

(b) He wanted to use elephants for circus.

(c) He wanted to defeat the Quraish because they travel too much.

(d) He wanted to destroy the Ka'bah so that people would go to Yemen.

3. What creature ultimately stopped Abrahah from his plan?

....

4. How was the army of Abrahah ultimately destroyed? (circle the correct answer)

   (a) A hurricane destroyed them.
   (b) Lots of birds ate up their grain.
   (c) Lots of birds knocked out the army with stones of baked clay.
   (d) The elephants trampled all the army.

5. From which place did Abrahah come to Makkah?

   (a) From Mesopotamia in the North.
   (b) From Yemen in the South.
   (c) From Egypt in the West.
   (d) From Alexandria in the West.

6. Who was the leader of the Quraish when Abrahah came to attack Makkah?

   (a) Abdullah.
   (b) Abdul Muttalib.
   (c) Abu Bakr
   (c) Abu Lahab

7. What was the reason the Quraish did not fight the army of Abrahah?

   (a) Abrahah gave them money not to fight.
   (b) Abrahah imprisoned all the leaders of the Quraish.
   (c) The Quraish were afraid of the large army, and they believed they had no power to defeat Abrahah.
   (d) The Quraish army was away in Yemen.

8. Which famous Quraish was born in the same year Abrahah came to attack Makkah?

   (a) Umar ibn Al-Khattab
   (b) Muhammadﷺ
   (c) Abdul Muttalib
   (d) Khadijah

9. Color the animal.

On the line below, write the Arabic word for elephant.

_____

- - - - - - - - - - - - - - - - - - -

_____

10. Abrahah took a difficult path to reach Makkah. Trace the path in the maze to reach the Ka'bah.

11. Unscramble the following to make meaningful words.

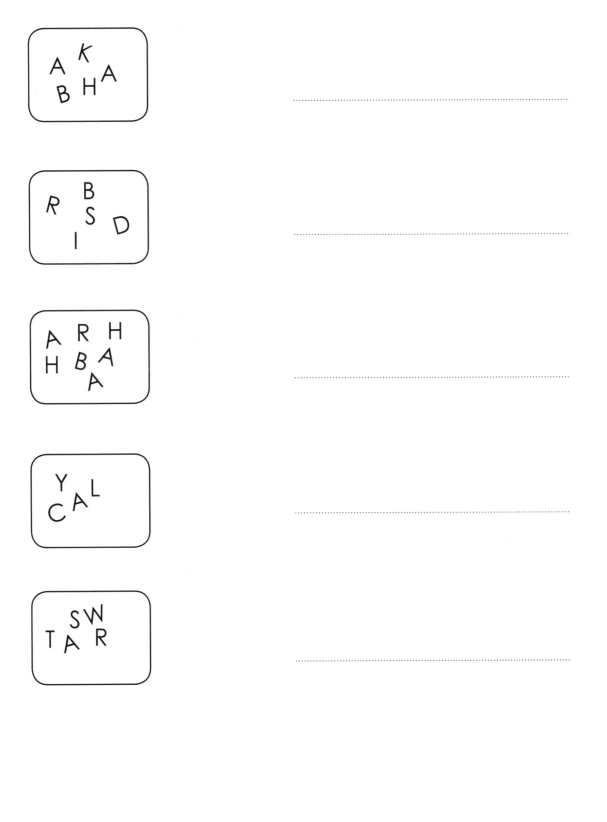

A K B H A ....

R B S D I ....

A R H H B A A ....

Y C A L ....

S W T A R ....

Sūrah 104

Al-Humazah

The Slanderer

Review **Summary**

This sūrah talks about the two types of sins common among people:

1. Talking bad about others behind their back.

2. Collecting money and not sharing it with the poor.

People not only talk bad behind other's back, they also spread slander. Slander means to spread lies about a person to make him or her look bad in front of others.

This sūrah criticizes them because of their bad conduct and cautions them about severe punishment in the Hereafter. The sūrah also reminds us that if we behave badly, then we will also face severe punishment. Allāh﷾ dislikes people who save money but never spend wealth on a good cause. Allāh﷾ dislikes people who say terrible things, spread false rumors, back-bite, and call others bad names.

Review **Questions**

1. What are the two sins mentioned in the first āyah of sūrah Humazah?

....

2. The second āyah of sūrah Humazah describes some activities of the person. What does he do?

....

3. What does the greedy people hope to get by collecting wealth?

....

4. What will be punishment for the sins mentioned in sūrah Humazah?

....

5. Which part of the body will be burning in fire, as mentioned in sūrah Humazah?

....

6. In sūrah Humazah, the severity of torment is stated in a certain manner. Circle which of the following statement is correct about nature of the torment.

   (a) The torment would be of extremely cold environment.
   (b) The torment would be of poisonous snakes.
   (c) The torment would be of massive landslide.
   (d) The torment would be crushing in nature.

7. In āyah 4 of sūrah Humazah, a special word is used to denote severity of torment. Write the Arabic word of this torment.

....

8. Burning fire can have different shapes. Āyah 9 of sūrah Humazah states the fire would be of certain shape. Circle which of the following description is correct.

   (a) It would be circular in shape.
   (b) It would be columnar in shape.
   (c) It would be sparkling in shape.
   (d) It would be like a candle flame.

9. What Arabic word is used in sūrah Humazah to CANCEL the idea previously stated?

   (a) ٱلَّذِى

   (b) أَنَّ

   (c) كَلَّا

10. Complete the puzzle using the clues below.

Across:

1. The first word of sūrah Humazah.
2. The organs of sinners that will burn.
4. To throw.
5. This will be kindled for the sinners.

Down:

1. This will not benefit the sinners. Riches.
2. To store. The sinners do this with their wealth.
3. Speak lies against others to damage their reputation.

11. Color the two dollar bills. Then cut them. Write four different characteristics of the person mentioned in sūrah Humazah in the front and back of the bills.

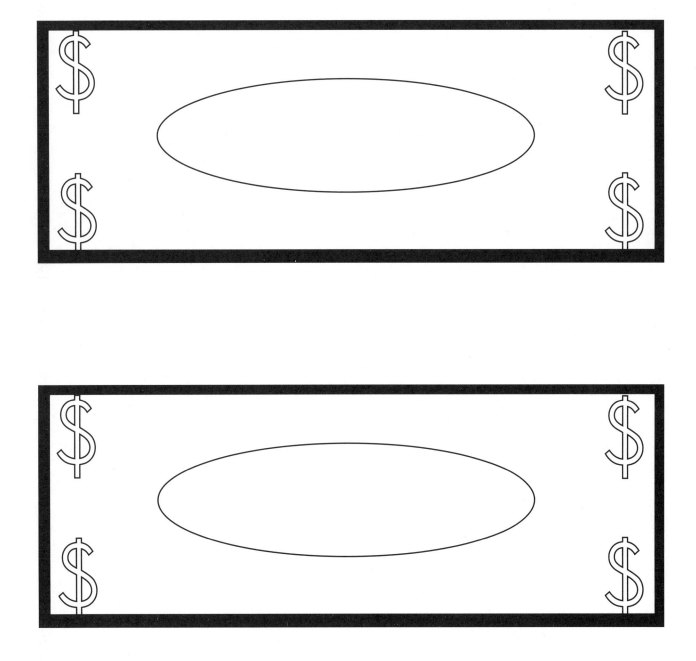

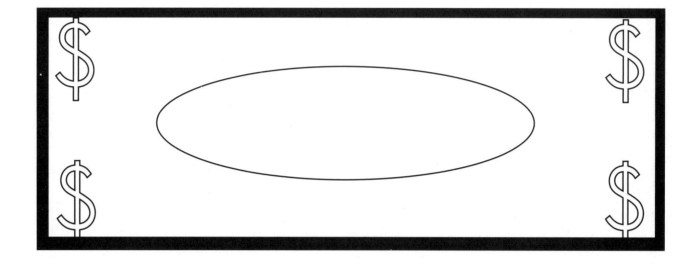

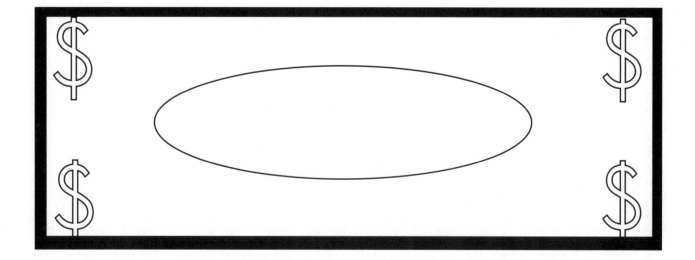

Sūrah 103

Al-'Asr

The Declining Day

Review **Summary**

The Arabic word 'Asr means "time" or "afternoon" or "declining day." The companions of Rasūlullāhﷺ would recite the sūrah before leaving each other's company.

Allāh﷾ begins the sūrah by declaring that as time passes, everyone eventually will be lost in this life except those who do four important things:

1) Believe in God

2) Do good deeds

3) Guide and encourage others to the truth of Islam

4) Guide and encourage others to be patient

Review **Questions**

1. According to sūrah al-'Asr, who will be at loss?

   (a) Companion of Rasūlullāhﷺ .
   (b) One man.
   (c) All men, but not all women.
   (d) All men and women.

2. What Arabic word is used in sūrah al-'Asr to indicate loss?

   (a) ٱلْإِنسَـٰنَ

   (b) خُسْرٍ

   (c) عَمِلُوا۟

3. Based on sūrah al-'Asr, write four things we should do so as not to suffer loss but be winner.

1. ....

2. ....

3. ....

4. ....

4. In sūrah al-'Asr, one word is mentioned twice. Write which of the Arabic word is repeated and its meaning.

_____   ....

- - - - - - - - - - - - - - - -

_____   ....

(Arabic word)   (meaning)

5. Write the meaning of the following words:

ءَامَنُوا۟   ....

عَمِلُوا۟   ....

ٱلصَّٰلِحَٰتِ   ....

6. Clocks on the left have Arabic words and the clocks on the right have their meanings. Draw lines to connect the clocks with words to their correct meanings.

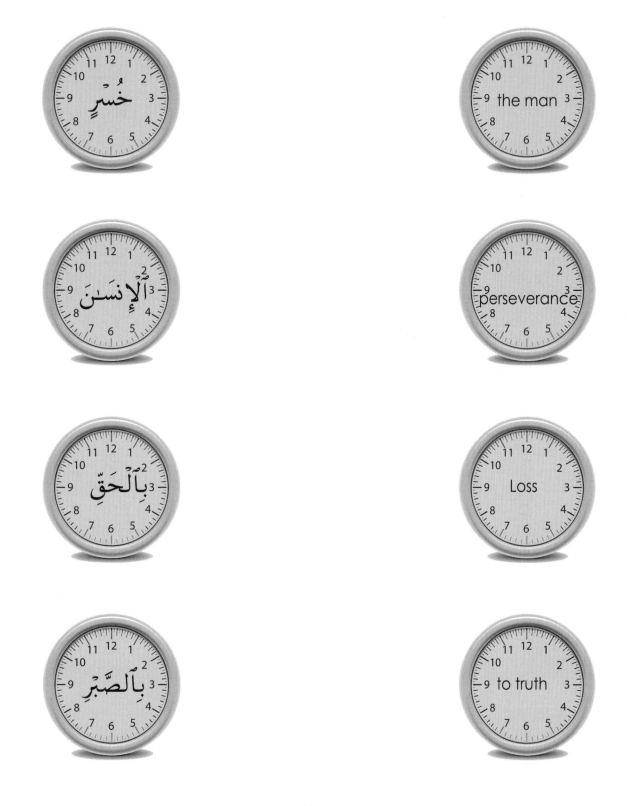

9. Find the following words in the word maze. Search the words in all directions, including backwards and diagonally.

time	loss	believe	good	encourage
success	truth	enjoin	perseverance	practice

```
E  M  I  T  E  L  X  M  T  B  U  I
J  P  Y  B  N  O  O  T  H  G  E  P
X  A  W  L  J  S  T  R  V  O  G  H
F  E  P  G  O  S  A  G  L  O  A  R
J  B  E  L  I  E  V  E  T  D  R  S
S  T  I  P  N  S  S  E  C  C  U  S
X  T  X  P  Y  W  U  X  W  Y  O  N
P  E  R  S  E  V  E  R  A  N  C  E
J  T  L  U  C  G  D  X  A  C  N  L
N  R  H  A  T  V  J  F  K  H  E  U
T  Q  D  P  Q  H  G  N  A  A  P  C
M  N  P  R  A  C  T  I  C  E  U  C
```

Bonus word: **surah** (diagonal)

Sūrah 102 | At-Takāthur

The Multiplication

Review Summary

Large number of people want to collect money and wealth all their lives. People think success in this world is all about how much wealth a person collects. These people are distracted from the real purpose of life. Only when people die, they will realize they wasted their lives in useless activities. The real purpose of life is to be successful in the Hereafter. When people will see the flaming fire, they will realize it was a mistake to ignore the Hereafter.

The message of sūrah At-Takāthur is a warning to these people who spend their life collecting wealth and ignore the real purpose of life.

Review Questions

1. What is the meaning of "multiplication" in the first āyah of sūrah Takāthur?

   ....

2. When do people realize accumulating wealth was not a good idea?

   ....

3. Āyat 3 and 4 repeats "you will soon know." What will people soon know?

   (a) That people should become poor before death.
   (b) That people should not collect any wealth at all.
   (c) That wealth should not divert people from remembrance of Allāh.
   (d) That people should collect small amounts of wealth to prevent being noticed.

4. Fill in the blanks using appropriate words in the box.

> selfishly   diverts   worship   souls   warnings
>
> accumulate   objective   graves

The tendency to amass wealth .... a person from his or her

good sense. The real objective of life should not be to ....

wealth, but to do good and .... Allāh. People who

.... accumulate wealth do not realize the real

.... of life until they are about to die. At that time and after

their death, their .... realize that wealth has no value in

the Hereafter. When they are in their ...., their souls will

realize they missed the real opportunities in this life. People who do not pay attention

to these .... will surely recognize the consequences. Only

then will they believe. Then they will see the punishment that lies ahead.

5. Write the meaning of the following words:

ٱلْمَقَابِرَ   ....

ٱلْيَقِينِ   ....

ٱلْجَحِيمَ   ....

6. What is the true purpose of life?

....

7. What is the meaning of the root word "Kathura", from which the title of the sūrah is derived? (circle the correct choice)

   (a) To know for sure
   (b) To multiply
   (c) To see clearly
   (d) To divert

8. The word "ilm-al-yaqin" used in āyah 5 means: (circle the correct choice)

   (a) Knowledge of Akhirah
   (b) Knowledge of uncertainty
   (c) Knowledge of certainty
   (d) Knowledge of graves

9. Read the āyah 8 of sūrah Takāthur. What is the meaning of the last word in that āyah?

   (a) Multiplication
   (b) Knowledge
   (c) Competition
   (d) Blessings

10. Sūrah Takāthur speaks about something that sinners will most certainly see. What will they see?

   (a) Tears in their eyes
   (b) Shadow
   (c) Fierce fire
   (d) Rivers of paradise

11. Sūrah Takāthur says the sinners will be questioned about something. About what will they be questioned?

   (a) Wealth—how did they use it.
   (b) Paradise—when they want to enter.
   (c) Children—how did they educated them.
   (d) Fire—how do they want it ignited.

12. Unscramble the following to make meaningful words.

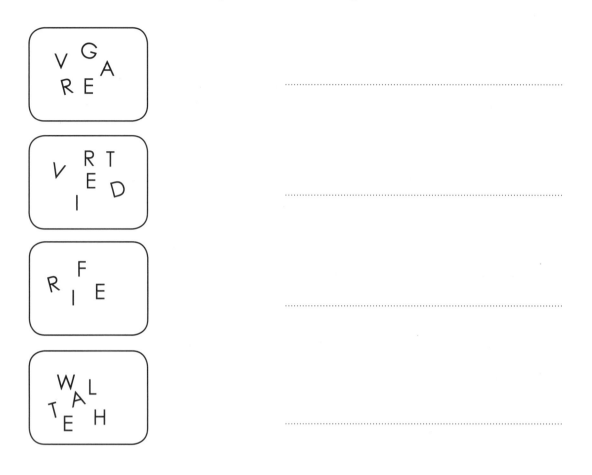

....

....

....

....

13. Find as many words of three or more letters from this wordwheel. Form words by using the letter in the center of the wheel plus a selection from the outer wheel. No letters may be used for more than once in a word.

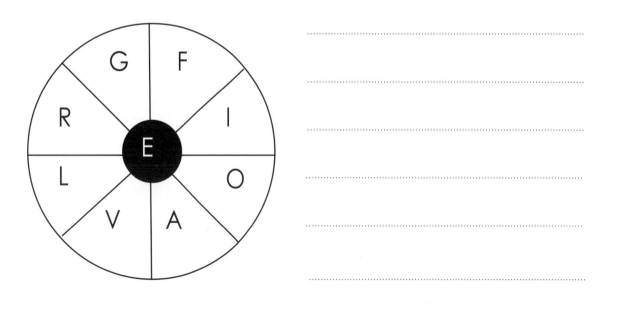

....

....

....

....

....

Sūrah 101

Revealed in Makkah

Al-Qāri'ah

The Disaster

Review Summary

This sūrah describes the terror of the Day of Awakening. People will be scattered and confused just like moths flying from place to place without a clear direction. The mountains will not be solid any more. They will be like scattered of wool.

On this day everyone's deeds will be weighed on a scale. Those whose good deeds are heavier than their bad deeds will be rewarded with paradise, and those whose bad deeds are heavier than their good deeds will be punished in Hellfire.

Review Questions

1. What is the English meaning of sūrah al-Qāri'ah?

....

2. On the Day of Awakening, the condition of mankind is compared with an insect. What insect is mentioned in sūrah al-Qāri'ah?

....

3. Why mankind is compared with that insect? What will happen to them?

....

....

4. On the Day of Awakening, what will happen to the mountains?

....

5. Write a list of things that will make the balance heavy with GOOD deeds.

....

....

....

....

6. List some things that would make the balance heavy with BAD deeds.

....

....

....

....

7. If the balance of deeds is light for a person, that person will be in some place. What is that place?   (circle the correct answer)

(a) He will be in hot spring

(b) He will be in an abyss

(c) He will be in deep mud

(d) He will be in rotten dumpster

8. The person whose scale is light, his destination will be at some place. What will that place be like to him?

    (a) It will be like his school

    (b) It will be like his mother

    (c) It will be like a cruise ship

    (d) It will be like a raised throne

9. Write the meanings of the following words:

كَٱلْفَرَاشِ   ....

ٱلْمَبْثُوثِ   ....

ٱلْجِبَالُ   ....

مَوَازِينُهُۥ   ....

10. Unscramble the following to make meaningful words.

O M T H S   ....

L A B A E C N   ....

11. Find the following words in the word maze. Search the words in all directions, including backwards and diagonally.

QARIAH	CALAMITY	MOTHS	SCATTER	MOUNTAIN
WOOL	BALANCE	LIGHT	HEAVY	ABYSS

Y V E O M O U N T A I N

B H A I R A Q P O D Y G

A Y T I M A L A C X H E

N B O U U V S Y F B J C

J W Y Q J C L P I L Q N

R D Y S A D I B H A W A

U D D T S R G Z E Z G L

Y B T V U S H B A I I A

U E W P H E T Q V N G B

R W G T W D P Q Y G L W

H L O O W I C Y E P A Y

K M V R Q W L A B R W J

Bonus word: **BLAZING**

Sūrah 100 | Al-'Ādiyāt

Revealed in Makkah

The Attackers

Review Summary

This sūrah continues with the reminder that people should prepare for the Day of Awakening. The opening verse describes the situation when invaders on horseback attacked a village in the middle of the night. The sudden chaos of the attack is similar to when people will be awakened on the Day of Judgment. The sūrah goes on to speak about man's love for this life and for the collection of wealth.

The sūrah concludes with a warning of the final day; the day when graves will scatter with all that lay within them. It warns us of the day when the deepest secrets that man hid within himself will be exposed.

Review Questions

1. Mention some of the images the galloping horses create in the first five āyāt of sūrah al-Ādiyāt.

....

....

....

....

....

2. Ayāh 6 of sūrah al-Ādiyāt reminds us of certain behavior of people. What is that behavior?

ungrateful to his Rabb

3. What is one of the reasons some people are ungrateful to their Creator?

man becomes greedy

4. Fill in the blanks using appropriate words in the box.

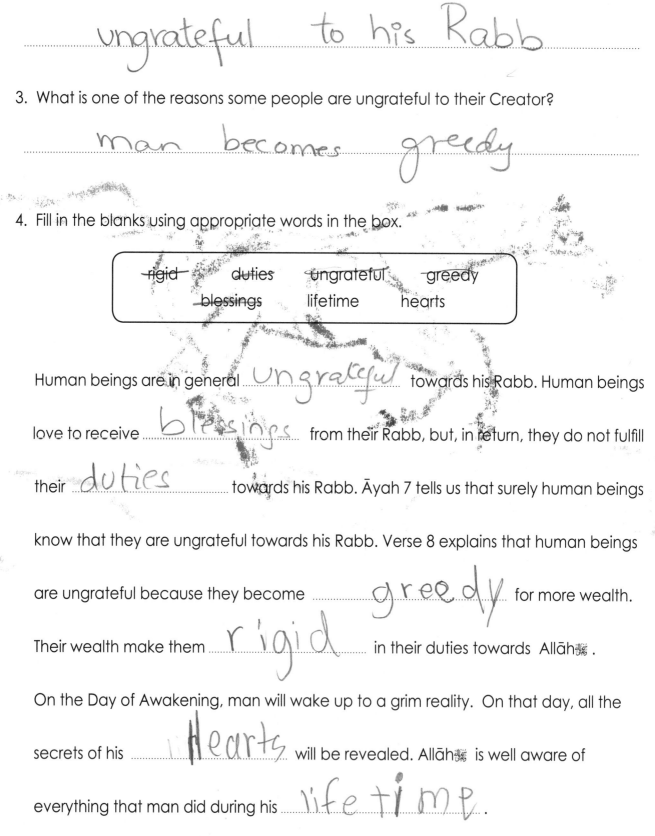

| ~~rigid~~ | duties | ~~ungrateful~~ | ~~greedy~~ |
| ~~blessings~~ | lifetime | hearts |

Human beings are in general _Ungrateful_ towards his Rabb. Human beings

love to receive _blessings_ from their Rabb, but, in return, they do not fulfill

their _duties_ towards his Rabb. Āyah 7 tells us that surely human beings

know that they are ungrateful towards his Rabb. Verse 8 explains that human beings

are ungrateful because they become _greedy_ for more wealth.

Their wealth make them _rigid_ in their duties towards Allāh .

On the Day of Awakening, man will wake up to a grim reality. On that day, all the

secrets of his _Hearts_ will be revealed. Allāh is well aware of

everything that man did during his _lifetime_.

5. Write the meanings of the following words:

صُبْحًا   Snorting

لَكَنُودٌ   Ungrateful

لِحُبِّ   in love of

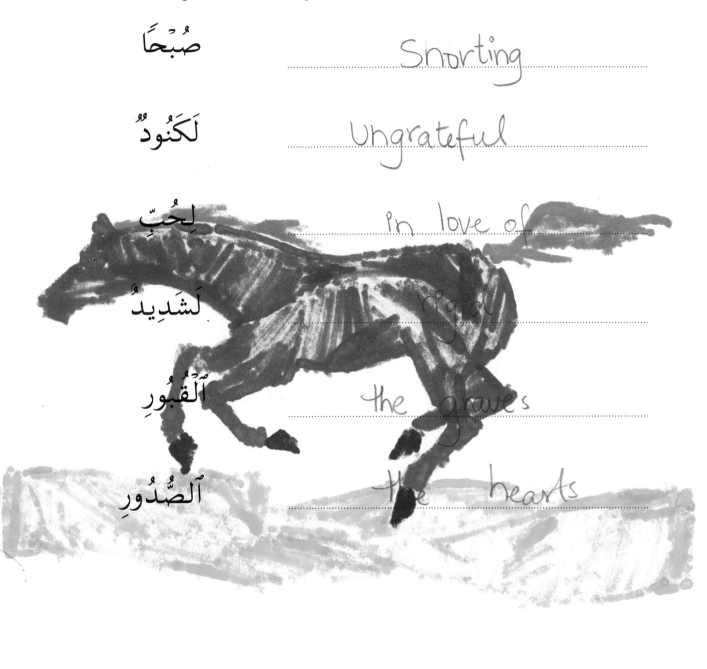

لَشَدِيدٌ

ٱلْقُبُورِ   the graves

ٱلصُّدُورِ   the hearts

6. Color the galloping horse.

7. Sūrah al-Ādiyāt begins with an oath on horses. What type of horses are they?

galloping

Sūrah 99

Az-Zalzalah

The Quake

Review Summary

This sūrah also briefly, but vividly, describes the Day of Awakening. Previously sūrah al-'Ādiyāt, al-Qāri'ah and at-Takāthur carried a similar message of preparing for the Final Day.

Sūrah Az-Zalzalah describes a terrifying earthquake will shake up the world on the Day of Awakening. On that Day the earth will open and push out all of the treasures, and anyone who ever lived. The people will be questioning what happened to the earth.

Allāh﷾ will inspire the earth to speak. The earth will then testify or show the evil actions that were done on it. The people will see every action that was done (even the smallest) and will be punished or rewarded based on their deeds.

Review Questions

1. What is the meaning of the word *zilzāl* ?

   earthquake

2. On the Day of Quaking, what will the earth do?

   The ground will be turned upside down and earth will bring out that is buried deep within

3. What will the earth relate on the Day of Quaking? Write the Arabic word for the term.

   Arabic word: zilzal

4. On that Day, why will people assemble in separate groups?

righteous groups & sinners group

5. On the Day of Awakening, what will both groups see?

The earth will reveal every human deed that it has witnessed

6. On the Day of Awakening, what will you want to see in large quantities?

7. Write the meanings of the following words.

أُخْرَجَتِ	brings out
ذَرَّةٍ	an atom
خَيْرًا	of good

8. Fill in the ovals with the names of some of the items that you think the earth will throw out on the Day of Judgment.

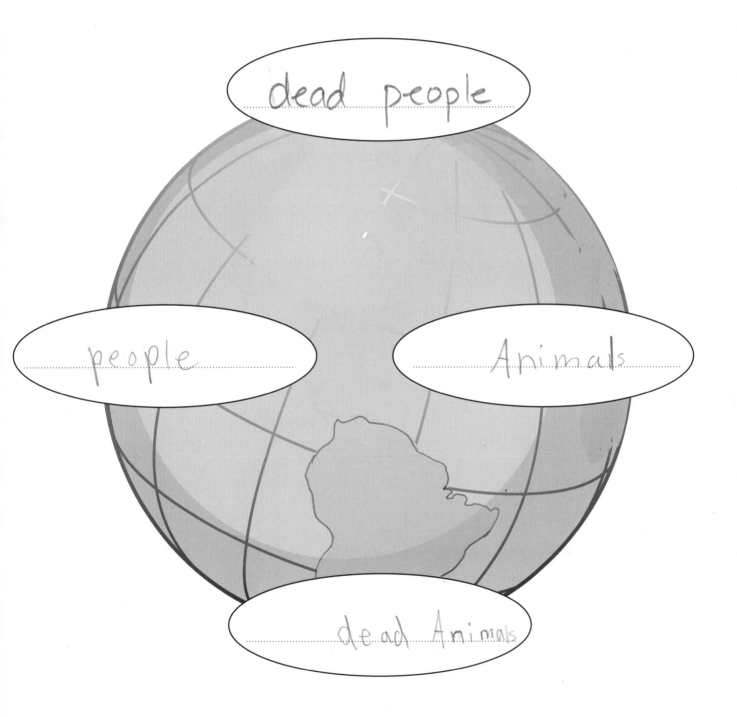

dead people

people

Animals

dead Animals

9. Fill in the blanks with the appropriate words given in the box.

~~atom~~   ~~turned~~   reward   separate   ~~shake-up~~
~~reveal~~   ~~punishment~~   ~~deeds~~

On the Day of Awakening, a sudden, terrible _Shake up_ of the earth

will happen. On that terrible day of shaking, the ground will be _Turned_

upside-down, and the earth will bring out all that is buried deep within. The earth will

reveal every human deed that it has witnessed. The righteous

people and the sinners will be brought in _separate_ groups. Every

person will see all of his or her _deeds_, even if it is as small as the

weight of an _atom_. Everyone will receive his or her due

rewards or _punishment_.

10. Unscramble the following to make meaningful words.

K Q A U E   _quake_

G W T I E H   _weight_

11. Color the eyes below and fill in each box with what the eyes see as good and bad deeds. Choose from the following list of actions.

salat ~~being kind~~ ~~lying~~ cheating respecting others
~~stealing~~ fasting ~~gossiping~~ remembering Allah
~~disobeying parents~~ ~~helping elders~~ ~~bullying~~

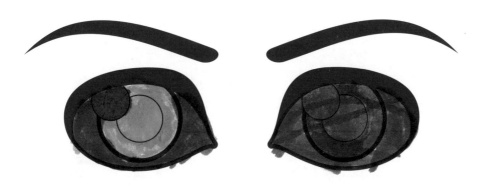

Good Deeds	Bad Deeds
Salat	Stealing
being Kind	disobeying parents
fasting	gossipping
helping elders	lying
Respecting others	cheating
remembering Allah	bullying

Sūrah 98

Al-Bayyinah

The Clear Proof

Review Summary

This sūrah describes the true believers are those who follow the Clear Proof (Qur'ān) and the Messenger. The People of the Book (Jews or Christians) or an idol worshippers should receive the Clear Proof through the pure pages of the Qur'ān so that they can follow the correct and straight path.

The believers were asked through all past messengers to do four main actions of the true religion:

1. To believe in Allāh
2. To worship Him with a sincere heart
3. Pray regularly
4. To give Zakāt, that is, to share one's wealth with others

It is now up to the People of the Book, and the idol worshippers to accept or reject the Clear Proof. Those who reject the truth are among the worst of creation, and surely deserve great punishment. Those who believe and do good deeds, they are among the best of creation and deserve a reward from their Rabb. Their reward is Paradise, in which rivers flow from underneath. Allāh will be pleased with them and surely they will remain in paradise forever.

Review Questions

1. Who are the People of the Book?

   Jews and Christans

2. What is the Clear Proof?

Allah will be pleased with them Just as they will.

3. The People of the Book were required to perform certain duties. What duties were they required to do?

....

....

....

4. Who are the worst of creation?

People Who Rejeects faith

5. Whoever rejects faith, from the People of the Book and polytheists; they will abide in some place. What is that place?

Ardah aahnnah

6. Which of the following statement is not true about the best of the creatures?

(a) They will be pleased with Allāh .

(b) They will be abide in Paradise for a short time.

(c) They believe and do good deeds.

(d) They establish salāt and pay zakāt.

7. Who will be well pleased and with whom?

(a) The People of the Book, with Allāh.
(b) The polytheists, with Rasūlullāh.
(c) The People of the Book, with Muslims.
(d) True believers, with Allāh.

8. Find a nine-letter snakeword hidden in the following grid. The nine letters form a continuous line passing through each cell once, without crossing itself.

Right path

9. Find as many words of three or more letters from this wordwheel. Form words by using the letter in the center of the wheel plus a selection from the outer wheel. No letters may be used for more than once in a word, except if a letter is present twice in the outer wheel.

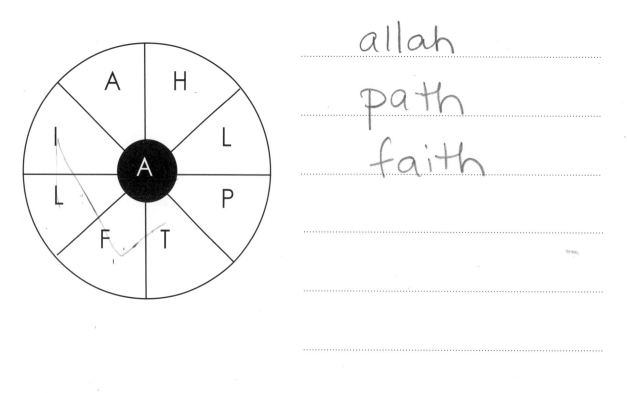

allah
path
faith

10. Allah﷾ sent many messengers to the People of the Book. Write the name of the book sent to each of the following messengers.

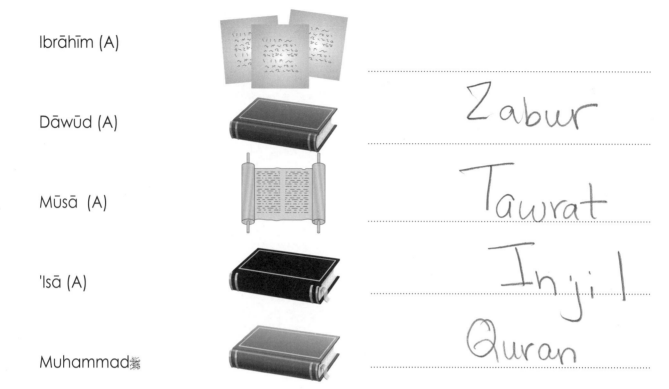

Ibrāhīm (A)

Dāwūd (A) — *Zabur*

Mūsā (A) — *Tawrat*

'Isā (A) — *Injil*

Muhammadﷺ — *Quran*

11. Read āyah 8. What Arabic word is used to name paradise?

12. In the description of paradise, which of the following phrase is used in sūrah Bayyinah?

   (a) Garden with abundant fruits.

   (b) Garden with shades of trees.

   (c) Garden with canopy, beneath which are carpets.

   (c) Garden, beneath which flow the rivers.

13. In āyah 5, two items from 5-Pillars of Islam are clearly mentioned. What are those?

   Zakat   *Salat*

14. Help the righteous teddy bear fill his heart with actions that you think has to be from the heart. Then color the teddy bear.

15. Connect each Arabic word to its English meaning.

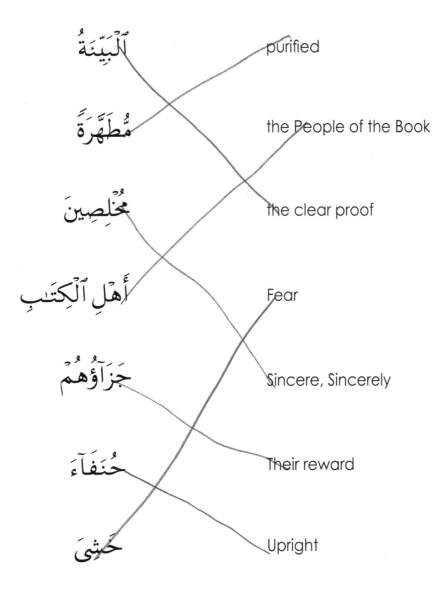

ٱلْبَيِّنَةُ	purified
مُطَهَّرَةً	the People of the Book
مُخْلِصِينَ	the clear proof
أَهْلِ ٱلْكِتَٰبِ	Fear
جَزَآؤُهُم	Sincere, Sincerely
حُنَفَآءَ	Their reward
خَشِىَ	Upright

Sūrah 97 | Al-Qadr

The Majesty

Review Summary

Laylatul-Al Qadr, or the Night of Power is the night that Angel Jibreel came to Rasūlullāhﷺ in Cave Hira with the first five āyāt of the Qur'ān.

The night of power is one of the odd-numbered nights of the last ten days in the month of Ramadan. It is a very important and holy night. In this night, every Muslim is encouraged to stay up all night or most of it to pray, and ask Allah for forgiveness and mercy.

It is truly a special night, it is peaceful and better than a thousand months. Angels come down with Angel Jibreel until the break of dawn.

Review Questions

1. In which month does Lailatul Qadar fall?

   Ramadan

2. On which night should we search for Lailatul Qadr?

   An odd number of night

3. Which āyāt were revealed in the night of al-Qadr?

   1 ayat

4. In which specific place the first five āyāt were revealed?

Cave Hira Known as Jabal an Nur

5. What is the name of the mountain where the first five āyāt were revealed?

Jabal an Nur

6. What three things happen every year on that very special night of Qadr?

(1) Angels, will descend to earth with permission of Allah

(2)

7. The night of majesty is better than how many days or months or years? (circle the correct answer)

(a) 100 months.
(b) 1,000 days.
(c) 1,000 months
(d) 10,000 months

8. Until what time the peace lasts on the night of majesty? (circle the correct answer)

(a) Until all children go to bed.
(b) Until all stars fade.
(c) Until people finish salātul Tahajjud.
(d) Until the rising of dawn.

9. Find the following words in the word maze. Search the words in all directions, including backwards and diagonally.

MAJESTY	NIGHT	QADR	THOUSAND	MONTHS
ANGELS	PEACE	DAWN	RAMADAN	JIBRIL

T X F J Q C Q P E A C E

E E R I Y C B P R V S X

J Q A B F N I G H T E W

M U M R W Y I Z H G S A

O N A I D G C O R H M A

N W D L H H U T S A U N

T D A T S S D Q J S F G

H O N R A L O E D B T E

S N Y N N M S A L C A L

B O D H B T W N P Z D S

Y S N V Y N T Q A D R L

M K V X U R W D D X Y E

10 Follow the path of good actions that one should perform on Lailat Al-Qadr in order to enter paradise peacefully.

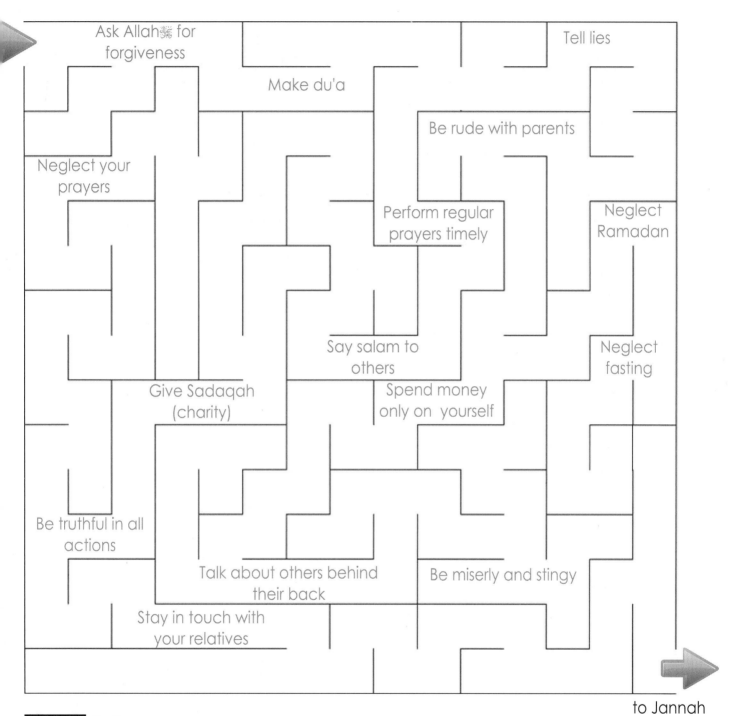

to Jannah

Think **Before you act**

What are some of the activities that would NOT take you to Jannah?

What are some of the activities that would take you to Jannah?

Other Popular Activity Books

These and many other books are designed for total learning success. Each book provides in-depth practice in skills required to excel in class. These books combine proven educational methods in exciting format to keep children interested to learn about Islam.

8.5" x 11", perfect bound, 96 pages

List price: $10.00
Discounts available.

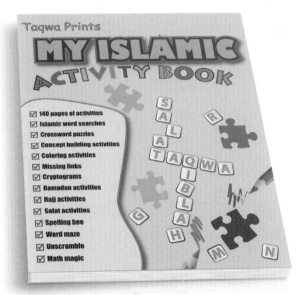

8.5" x 11", 160 pages

List price: $12.00
Discounts available.

8.5" x 11", Perfect Bound, 120 pages

List price: $10.00
Discounts available.

8.5" x 11", Perfect Bound, 128 pages

List price: $10.00
Discounts available.